My Super duper STICKER activity book

This book belongs to:

COdyTAlford

You'll find the stickers at the back of the book!

I'm Doodle Monster. Look out for me inside!

priddy 🙂 books

Quack, quack!

Find the missing stickers, then draw lines to match the birds.

Dino maze

Find the stickers, then help the baby dinosaur find its mum.

African animals

Find the animal stickers to complete this safari scene.

Buzzing about

Add the bug stickers to the flower.

Pirate trail

Find the stickers, then help the captain find his missing hook.

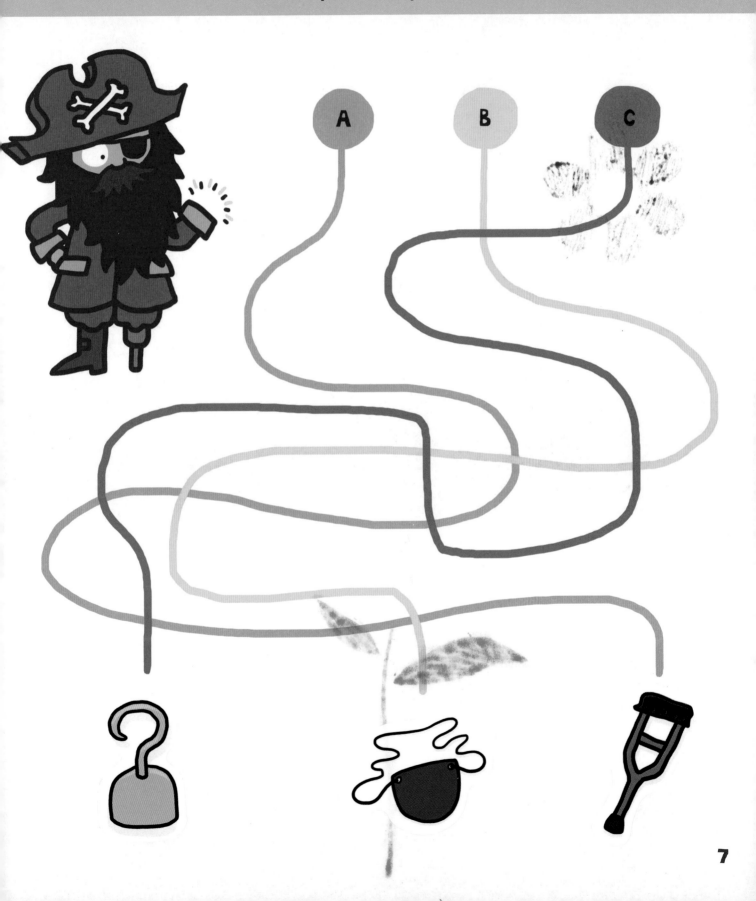

Flower garden

Find the missing flower stickers and add some bugs, too.

Can you colour in the flowers?

9

In the forest

How many fairies can you find hiding in the magical forest?

Crazy invention

Help Doodle Monster complete his doodle machine!

Terry's toolbox

Can you find the stickers to give Terry some tools?

Milk trail

Find the stickers, then help Farmer Claire find her pail.

Crowning glory

Find the stickers to crown these princesses.

Hide and seek

Find the stickers to show who's hiding in the dinosaur cave.

By the pond

Find the stickers to show who's by the pond today.

Three little pigs

Find the little pig stickers and get them safely home.

Teddy bears' picnic

Find the stickers to give these teddies some picnic treats.

Doodle, doodle

Complete the doodle lines!

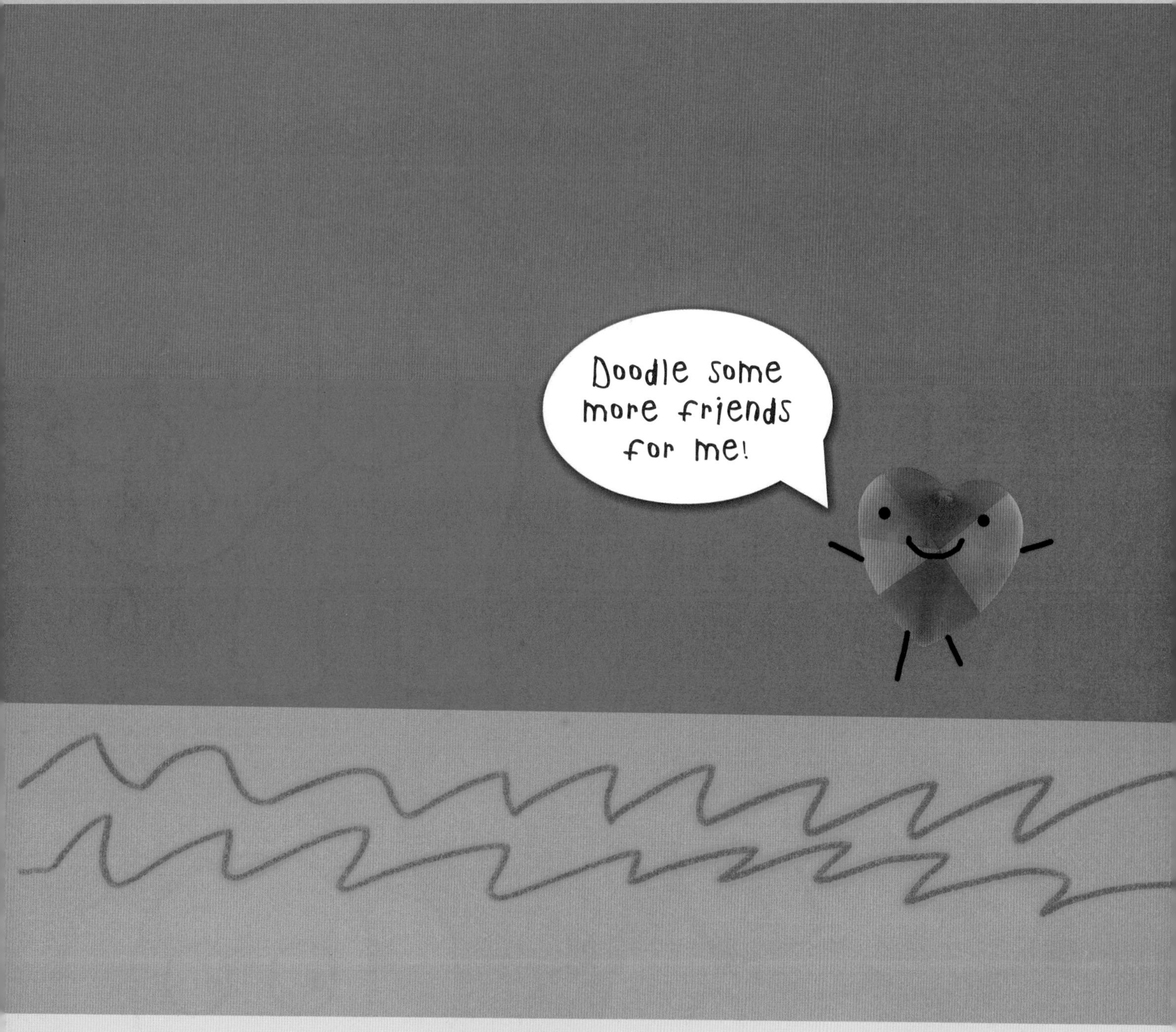
Doodle some more friends for me!

Splashing elephants

which elephant isn't splashing himself with water?

Counting carrots

How many carrots can you count in this picture?

Construction site

These builders are missing some important things.

Matching muffins

Find the stickers and draw lines between the matching pairs.

Lucy Ladybird

Can you find the stickers to give Lucy her spots?

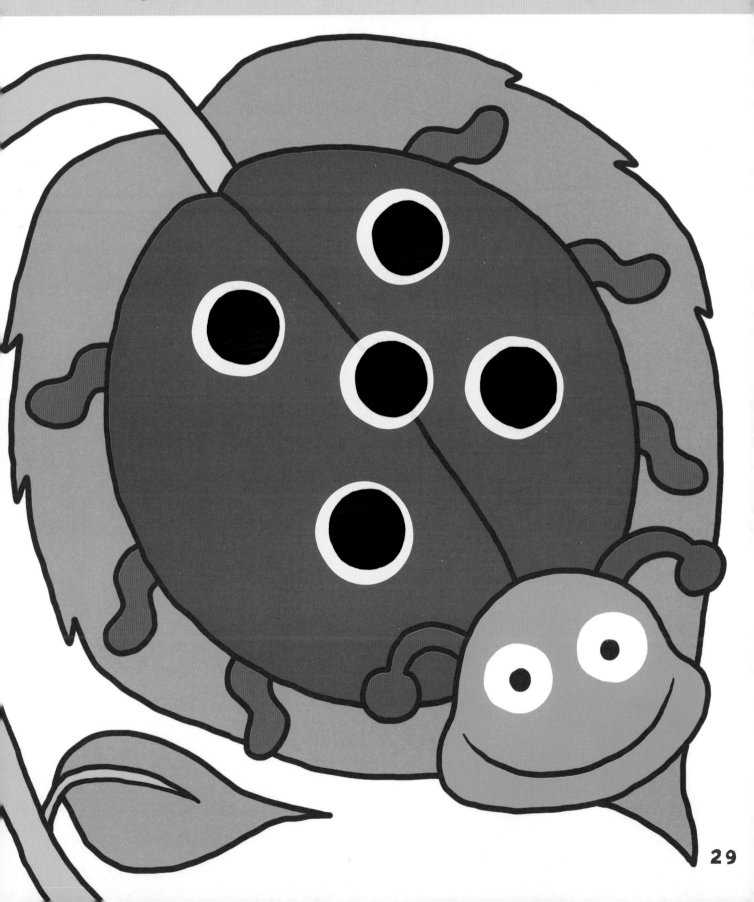

Monster's wardrobe

What's in Doodle Monster's wardrobe?

Colourful chicken

Colour in this picture of the chicken and the eggs.

Oliver the Owl

This owl wants to be really colourful!

Apple tree

Can you find the apple stickers to put on the tree?

The Frog Prince

Find the stickers, then help the princess find the Frog Prince.

Ship's deck

Who else is on board the pirate ship? Add the stickers.

Twinkling stars

Find the star stickers to complete this night-time scene.

In the jungle

Can you colour in this jungle scene?

Leaf creatures

Turn these leaves into friendly creatures!

Princess's bedroom

Use your stickers to decorate this pretty princess bedroom.

whose picture is on the wall?

Making faces

Find the stickers to complete the boy's face.

Happy families

Find the stickers, then match the mums to their babies.

Tool shed

Find the stickers that belong in Farmer Ted's shed!

What's missing?

The three hats and the wolf's tail are missing. Find the stickers.

Missing nails

Can you find the stickers to give the builders their nails?

Fairy Fiona

Can you find the stickers to give Fiona a smiley face?

Monster madness

Fill the page with lots of mini monsters!

Sweet treats

Count the red sweets then colour in the other treats.

Pretty sunflower

What colour is the sunflower?

Under the sea

Find the stickers to decorate the seabed.

Princess Penny

Can you find the stickers to get Penny ready for the ball?

Old MacDonald's farm

Find the animal stickers to fill Old MacDonald's farm.

what noises do the animals make?

Susie Stegosaurus

Can you find the stickers to give Susie her missing spikes?

In the harbour

Find the stickers to add to the harbour.

Harvest time

Can you find the stickers to complete the farm and fields?

where is the farmer?

Henry the Hedgehog

Give Henry lots of prickly spikes, then colour in the picture.

Summer holiday

which suitcase is the biggest?

Hairy monster

Doodle a face, arms and more hair!

Monster boxes

Turn these boxes into squary little monsters!

Builder's yard

Park the truck stickers in the builder's yard.

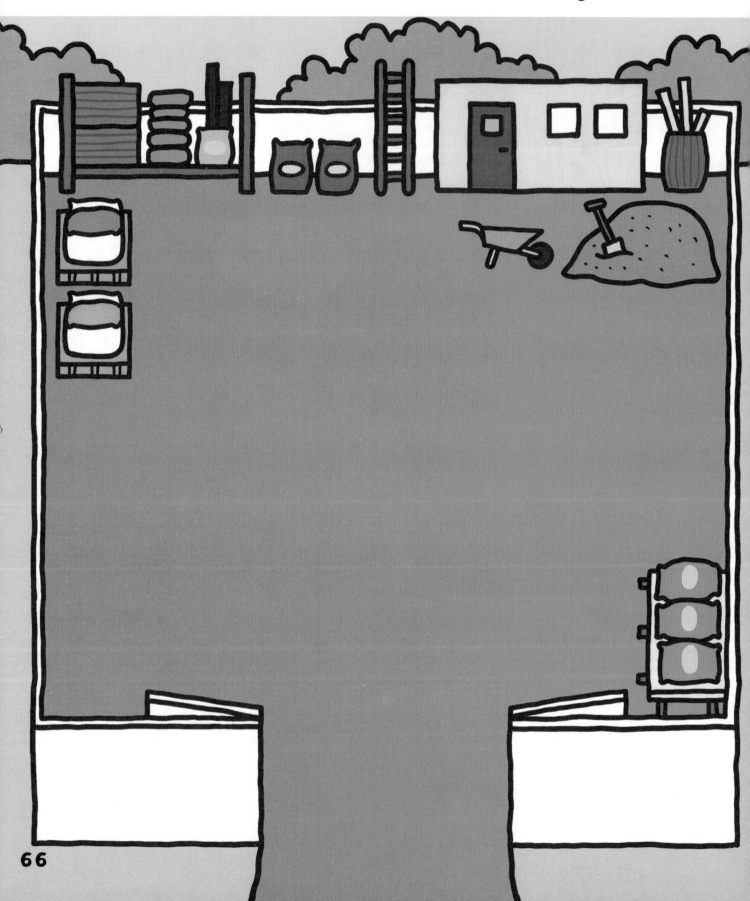

Love is in the air

decorate the sky with heart stickers.

Monkey trail

Find the stickers, then help the monkey find his snack.

Gingerbread house

Decorate the roof of the house with sweet stickers.

Secret cave

Find the stickers to decorate the pirate cave.

where will you put the bat stickers?

71

At the stables

Can you find the stickers of the pretty ponies?

Dino skeleton

Find the missing bone stickers to complete the picture.

73

Flower doodle

Keep drawing around this happy flower!

who will you put as the champion?

Join the dots to complete the crown, then colour it in!

In the trees

which orangutan is eating a banana?

Fairy kingdom

Find the stickers to decorate the fairy kingdom.

Can you find the fairy's frog friend?

The little dog

Find the stickers to complete the dog's face.

Barry's truck

Find the stickers to fill the builder's truck.

Tricky patterns

Can you complete these tricky doodle patterns?

Frosty family

Colour in the snow family. Don't forget little Tim!

Match and make

Match the builders with their materials!

saw

screwdriver

cement

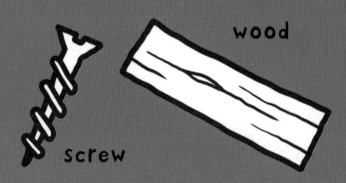

wood

nail

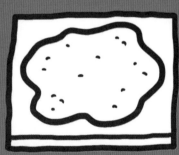

screw

trowel

hammer

Matching balls

Find the stickers, then draw lines between the matching balls.

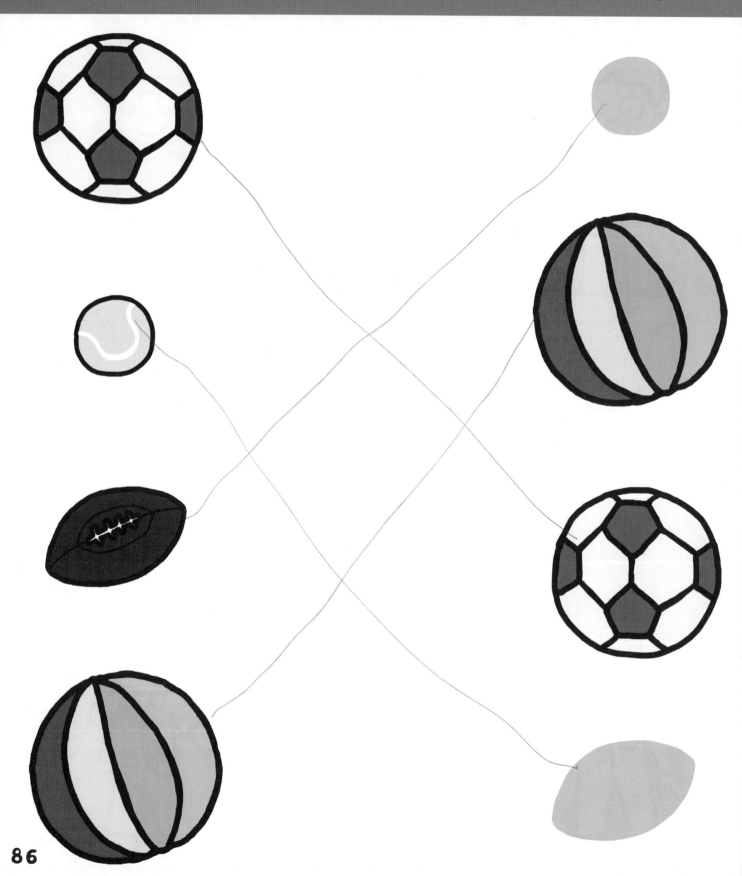

What's in the fridge?

Use your stickers to fill this fridge full of food.

Prehistoric land

Add your dinosaur stickers to this prehistoric scene.

Can you spot the dinosaur bone?

Matching sea life

Can you draw lines between the matching sea creatures?

Spotted cows

Spot the five differences between Daisy and Maisy.

Gingerbread friends

Finish off these gingerbread friends!

Flying fairies

Use your stickers to complete this magical scene.

X marks the spot

Find the stickers to put on the map.

Mermaid lagoon

Can you find the sea creature stickers?

Now colour in the palm tree!

Alien planet

Doodle your own alien planet.

who hangs out here?

what will you call your planet?

Gingerbread house

Can you find five differences between the two pictures?

Grand ball

Use your stickers to add guests to this beautiful ball.

Dino trail

Find the stickers, then help Dino Dave find his friend.

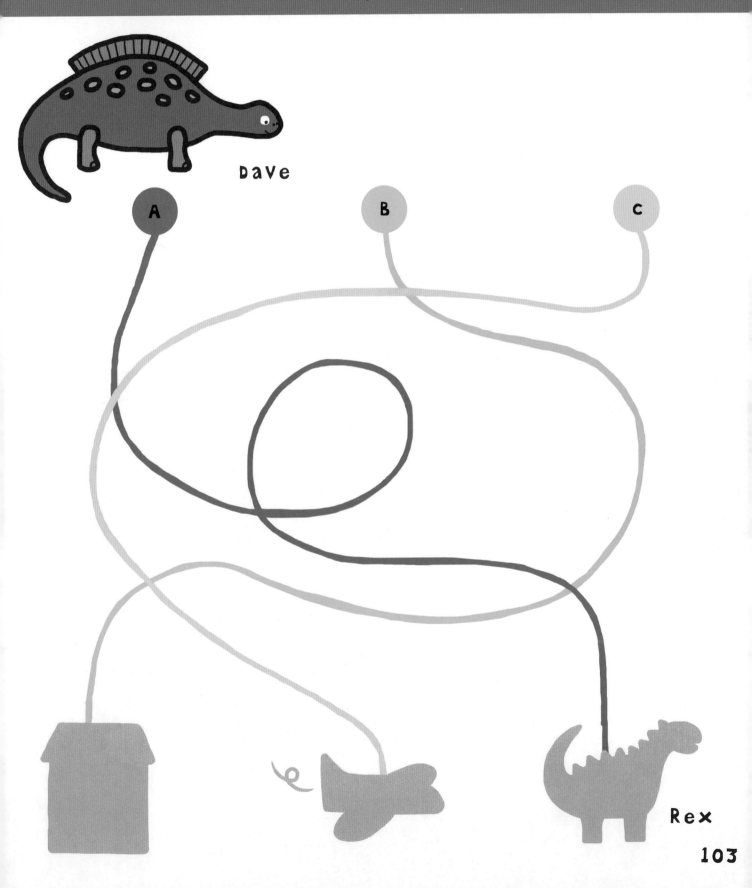

Dave

A   B   C

Rex

Muddy pig pen

Find the stickers to go in the pig pen.

Who's playing in the mud?

Palm pirates

Can you find the coconut stickers to put on the tree?

Berry bush

Add some berry stickers to the bush.

Dinosaur face

Use your stickers to give this T. rex a scary face.

Fairy castle

Add the flag stickers to this fairy castle.

Flower necklace

Can you give Sophie a pretty flower necklace?

The pantry

The cupboard is bare. Fill it with yummy food!

YUM!

Farm match

Draw lines between the pairs of matching farm characters.

Learn to draw

Can you copy this picture of a bulldozer? Now colour it in!

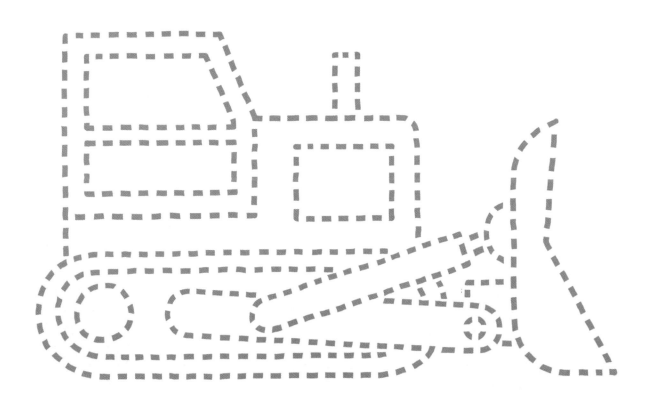

113

Toolbox trail

Find the stickers, then help Trevor find his toolbox.

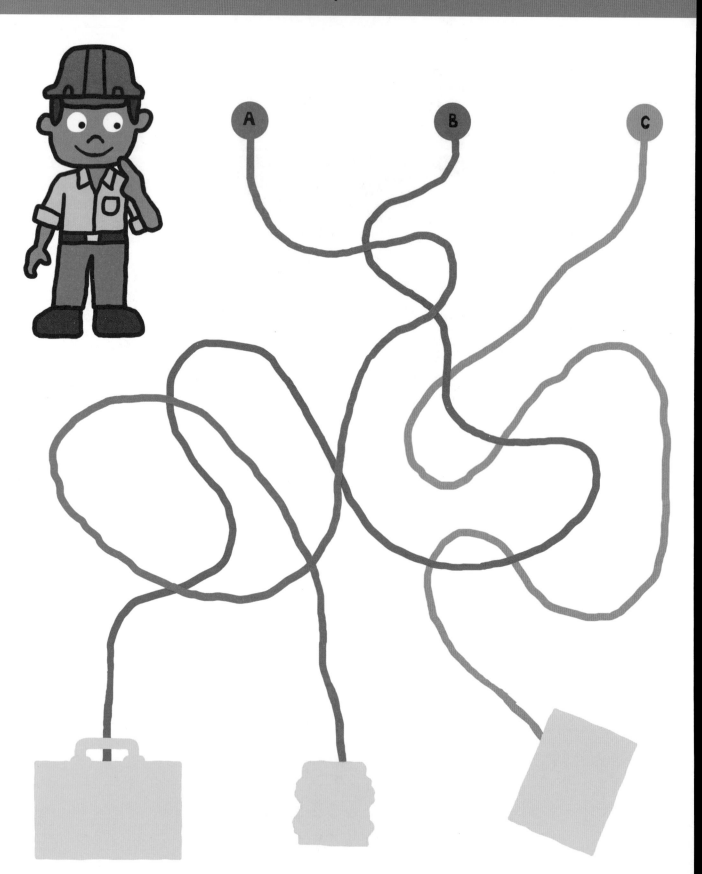

Picnic in the park

Can you find the stickers to make a tasty picnic?

Hot air balloons

Can you fill the sky with colourful hot air balloon stickers?

In the sky

Can you colour the smiley sun yellow?

118

The straw house

Can you spot the five differences between the pictures?

119

That's rubbish!

Turn the rubbish into something cool!

CHOO! CHOO!

Pretty ponies

Find the stickers, then match the princesses to their ponies.

122

Walk the plank

Can you find the stickers for this scary scene?

Construction city

Use your stickers to complete the city.

124

Can you colour in the park?

Meerkat madness

126

Hot desert land

Can you colour in the desert camels walking on the dunes?

128

Princess kingdom

Find the stickers to decorate the princess kingdom.

Busy bumblebee

Find the stickers, then help the bumblebee find his flower.

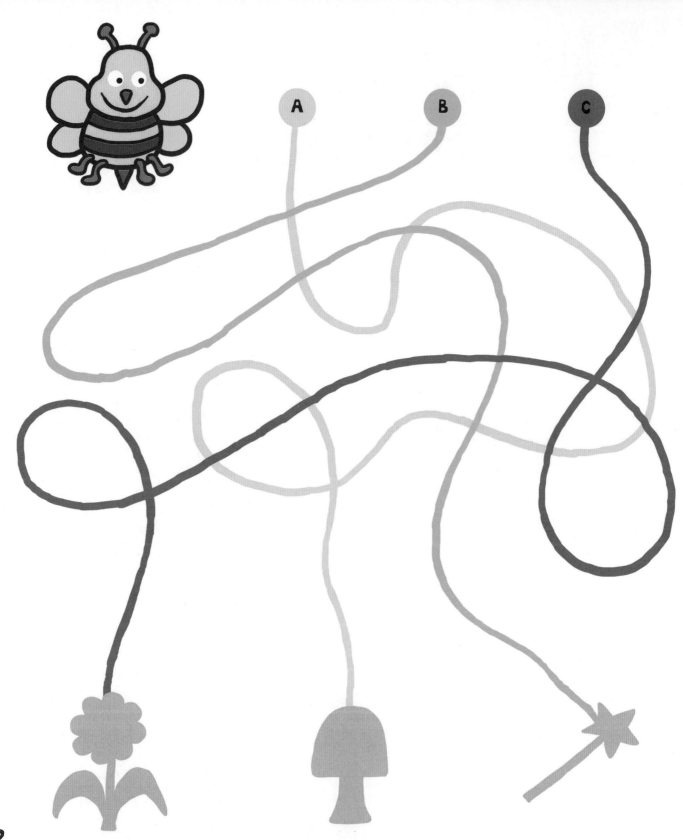

Volcano

Find the stickers to complete this prehistoric scene.

Woolly cardigan

Can you find the colourful buttons to decorate the cardigan?

Matching pairs

Find the stickers, then draw lines between the matching pairs.

Starry night

Find the stickers to decorate the night-time scene.

who is hiding behind the tree?

Candy stripes

Draw stripes on these candy canes.

Disco doodle

Fill the page with swirls and musical notes.

Giant flower

Colour in little Flo the fairy and her giant flower.

Brilliant bats

which bat has gone to sleep?

Ben the builder

Find the stickers to give Ben a smiley face!

My farmhouse

Can you find the stickers to decorate the farmhouse?

Crown jewels

Find the jewel stickers and decorate the crown.

144

Flying dinosaurs

Find the stickers to complete this scene.

Apartment block

How many windows are on the tower block?

Juicy fruits

Can you circle all of the apples?

147

Paint splodge zoo

Turn these paint splodges into animals.

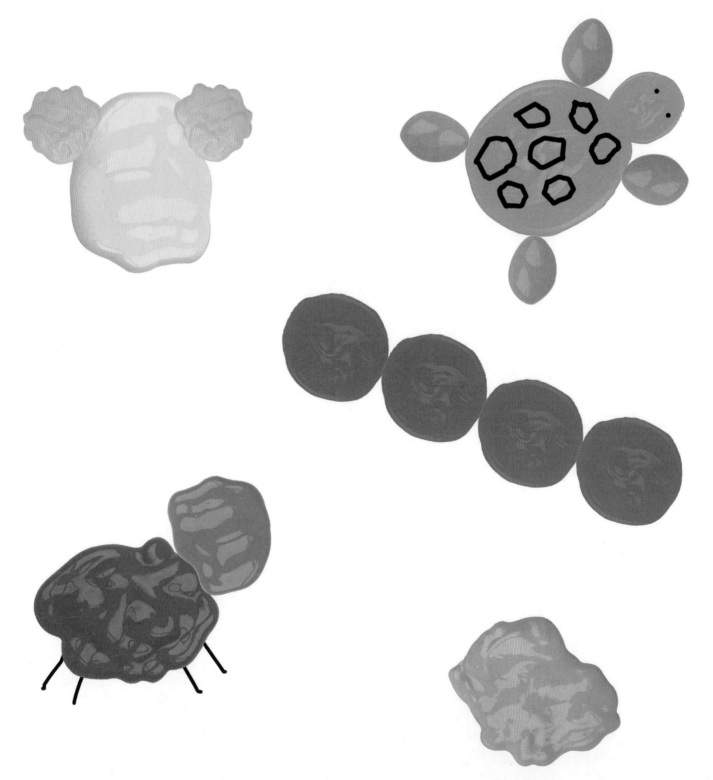

Flowerpot village

Find the stickers to decorate the flowerpot village.

Setting sail

Add the flag, anchor and cannon to this pirate ship.

Birthday cake

Why not decorate the cake with candle stickers?

Princess Lucy

Find the stickers to give Lucy a smiley face.

Royal doodles

These stick friends are all princes and princesses.

154

155

Sail away

Join the dots to complete the boat's sail and colour it in.

Spot the difference

Can you spot the five differences between these two fairies?

Lost mittens

Find the mitten stickers to keep the kittens warm?

Sheepdog maze

Find the stickers, then help the sheepdog find the sheep.

Desert island

Find the stickers to decorate the pirate island.

161

Picnic time

Find the stickers to give the fairies some picnic treats.

Missing tools

Can you find the stickers of these builders' tools?

Rhino Rob

Can you draw on Rhino Rob's missing horn?

Draw a shoe

Trace over the dotted line to draw a shoe, then colour it in!

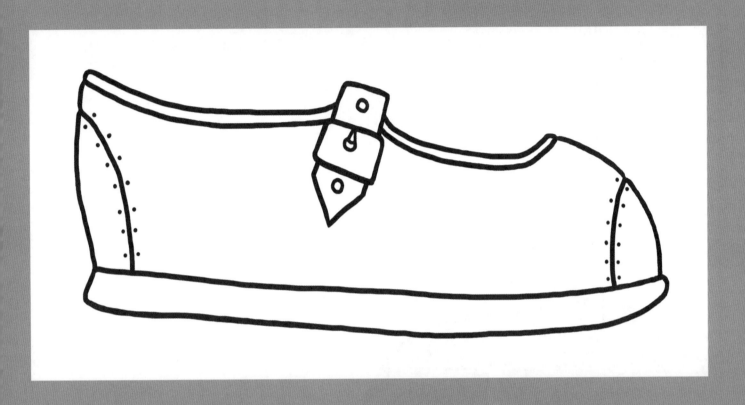

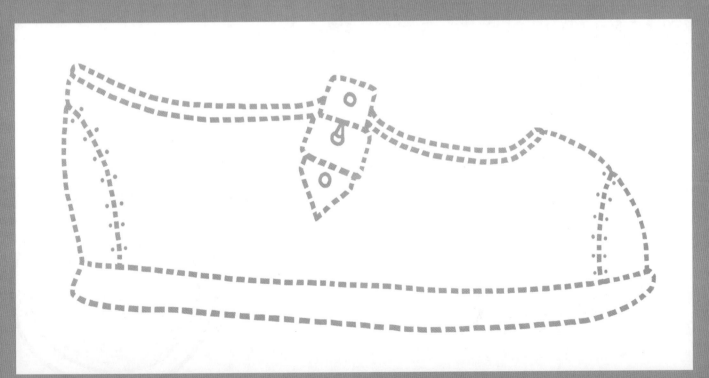

Perfect picnic

Doodle all the yummy food you would eat at a picnic!

Postcard

Doodle a really cool postcard design!

Under the sea

Find the stickers to show who's under the sea.

Colour in the seaweed.

169

Matching pets

Find the stickers, then draw lines between the matching pets.

Prince Charming

Find the stickers to get Prince Charming ready for the ball.

Treasure maze

Find the stickers, then help Jolly Roger find his treasure.

Eric the Elf

Use your stickers to give Eric a smiley face.

Flamingo beach

These pink birds need some legs.

175

Crazy chameleon

Use your crayons to choose Kevin the Chameleon's mood.

Odd one out

which princess has lost her hat?

Dandelion Farm

Find the stickers to show how busy the farm is today.

Leafy tree

Can you find some leaf stickers to add to the branches?

Happy builder

Find the stickers to give this builder a smiley face.

All things round

Use your crayons to colour in all the round objects.

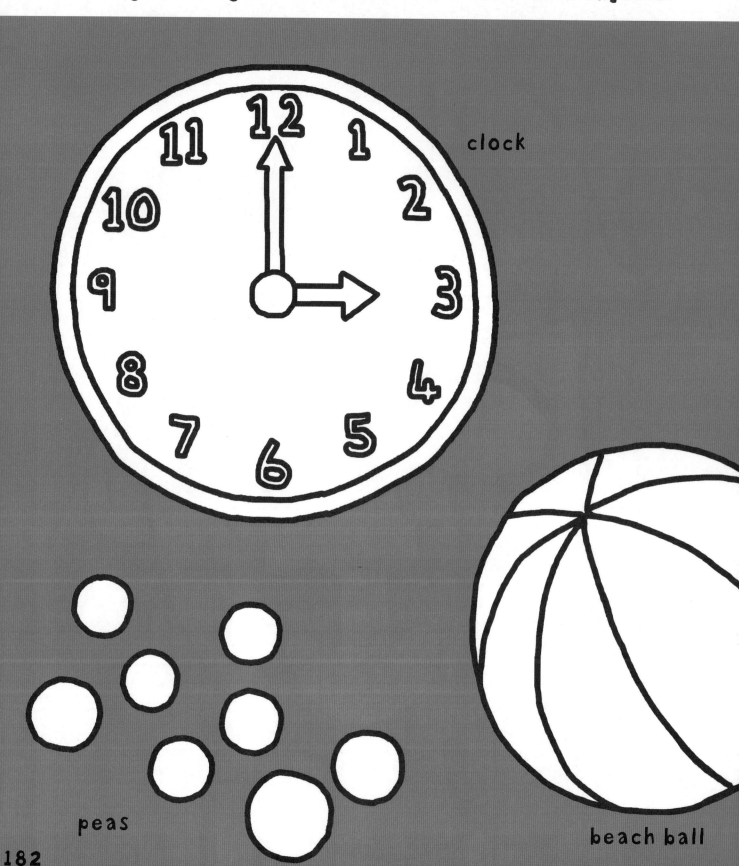

clock

peas

beach ball

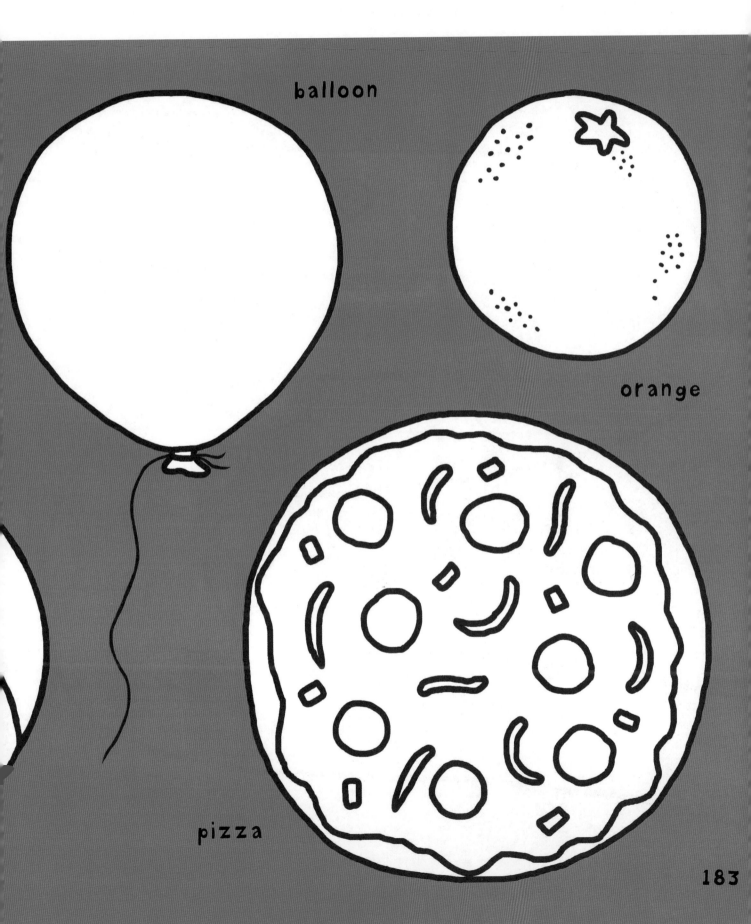

balloon

orange

pizza

183

Snail trails

Doodle cool patterns onto these snail shells!

which snail is the slowest?

Square doodle

draw around the little square and fill the page!

Rapunzel's bows

Use your stickers to add bows to Rapunzel's long hair.

Match the men

Find the stickers, then match the gingerbread men.

Blast off!

which stickers will you add to this space scene?

Big and small

Dinosaurs could be very big or very small. Find the stickers.

enormous

big

small

tiny

New York, New York

Koala Ken

Colour in Koala Ken. He loves to eat green eucalyptus leaves.

Pretty Pollys

Can you spot the five differences between the two parrots?

Cheese trail

Find the stickers, then help the mouse find his cheese.

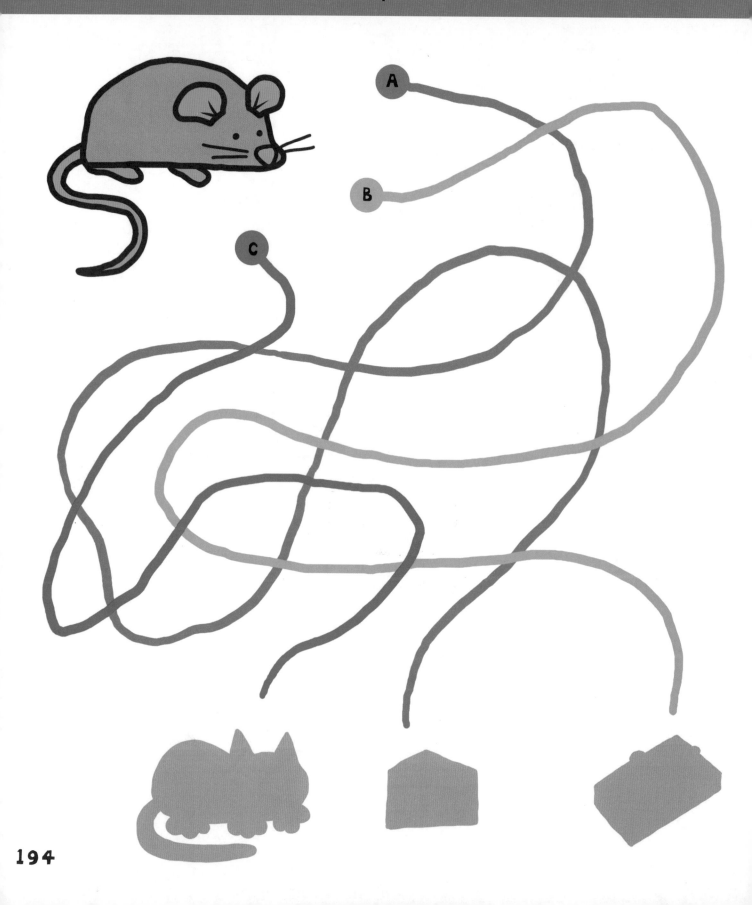

The muffin man

Can you find the stickers to complete the baker's face?

Cinderella

Add some flower stickers to Cinderella's pretty dress.

Haunted house

Find the stickers to make this house really spooky!

Princess bed

Can you draw some more mattresses to make the bed?

Learn to draw

Can you copy this picture of a Triceratops? Now colour it in!

Doodle champ
Decorate these ribbons!

No.1
doodle

Champ

Giant pie

Find another ten blackbird stickers to add to the scene.

Can you count the blackbirds?

Rex's trail

Find the stickers, then help Rex find the bone.

At the pond

can you find the stickers to decorate the fairy pond?

Roller coaster ride

doodle the rest of this roller coaster!

Fossils in the forest

How many fossils can you count?

209

Rain, rain, go away!

Can you find the missing raindrop stickers?

Missing hats

These people need hats! Can you find the stickers?

Monsieur cupcake

These cupcakes need faces and moustaches!

Draw it

What is Doodle Monster drawing?

Feathers

Doodle some more floating feathers around the page.

215

Rainbow colours

what colours are in your rainbow?

Magical maze

Help the fairy find her way to the castle.

Scary trail

Find the stickers, then help the prince get to the castle.

Scary scaffolding

Find the stickers to make this scaffolding safe!

Snowy day

Can you find the stickers to decorate the snowy scene?

Magical castle

How many cats can you count in the castle scene?

Creature features

Turn these blobs into crazy, creepy creatures!

name

Fart

Pete the Pirate

Find the stickers to give Pete a smiley face.

Buzzing about

Can you find the bee and honey stickers?

Time for tea

Find the stickers, then draw lines between the matching pairs.

Little ducklings

Use your stickers to add more ducklings to the pond.

Owl family

Draw the owl family hanging out in the treetops!

Cute hippos

Colour in these little hippos.

In the toy box

Can you circle all of the dolls?

233

Mad scientist's lab

Find the stickers to decorate this crazy scientist's laboratory.

Now colour in the monster!

Making faces

Find the stickers to make the girl's smiley face.

Vegetable garden

Use your stickers to plant vegetables in the garden.

Angelfish

These pretty fish swim in the Amazon River.

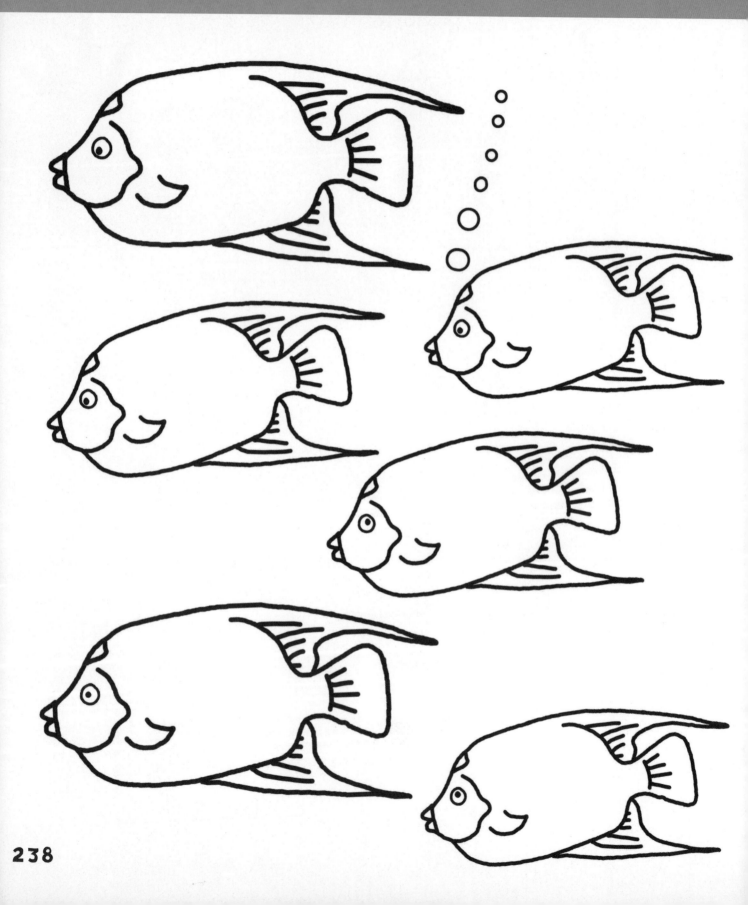

Matching pals

Can you draw a line between the matching builders?

Fluffy cat

Give Charlie the cat a super-fluffy body!

Time for tea

doodle pretty flowers on this teapot!

Prince Peter

Find the stickers to give Peter a smiley face!

Picnic in the park

Find the stickers to complete the park scene.

Captain club

Find the stickers to give these captains their hats.

Dinosaur family

Find the stickers to complete the dinosaur family.

Traffic jam

Make this traffic scene really busy!

ONE WAY

Tennis time

Which tennis player is holding a ball?

Fluffy chick

what colour is the fluffy chick?

Climb the beanstalk

Can you add some green leaf stickers to the beanstalk?

Mummies and babies

Find the stickers, then match the mums to their babies.

A wool trail

Find the stickers, then help the sheep find some tasty grass.

Treasure chest

Fill the treasure chest with stickers of golden objects.

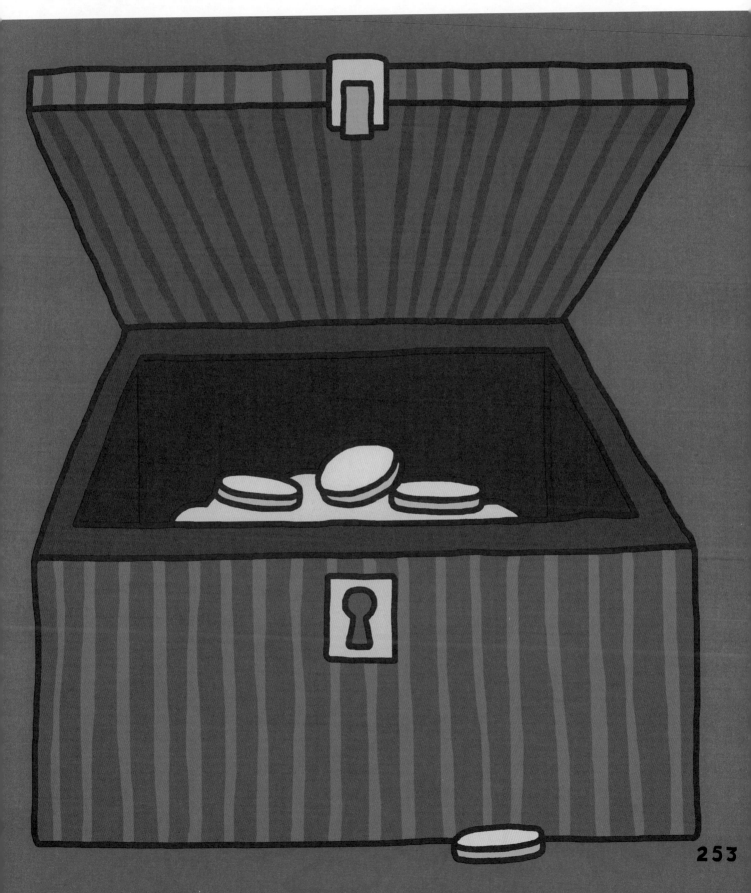

Witch's hat

Join the dots, then decorate the witch's hat.

Beautiful flowers

Make this big bunch of flowers lots of bright colours.

My town

Add windows, doors and cars!

Scary Mr Wolf!

Add some more teeth stickers to Mr Wolf!

Polar pals

Use your stickers to add more animal pals to this icy scene.

Monster pets

Doodle some really freaky pets!

Make them bald or furry, fat or thin, ugly or cute!

Pets at home

who is sleeping on the sofa?

263

In the sea

Find the stickers so the fish has lots of friends to swim with.

Farmer Bob

Can you find the stickers to give Bob a smiley face?

Dino trail

Find the stickers, then help this dinosaur find her babies.

Strawberry tart

Can you add more strawberry stickers to the tasty tart?

Help the prince!

Find the stickers, then help the prince find his princess.

Rhino trail

Which trail will lead the rhino to the grass?

Pirates in the jungle

Can you colour in the jungle scene?

It's a pizza

Doodle your favourite pizza topping.